Not Just Any Old Fruit: Picking the Fruit of the Spirit

Written and Illustrated by Emily Reagan

Joyful
Press Publishing

WHAT KIND OF FRUIT?

Just like fruit that grows on a tree, when you are learning more about Jesus and drawing closer to Him, you can develop fruit in your life too. How you behave and what you do every day shows what kind of fruit you are growing.

When you follow Jesus, your attitudes and actions reflect Him. To help you, Jesus gives you the gift of the Holy Spirit! The Holy Spirit is always with you as a helper.

There are nine specific things found throughout the Bible that are proof of the Holy Spirit in your life. The Apostle Paul listed these when he wrote a letter to the people of Galatia. This letter is the book of Galatians that you can read in your Bible today. This is the fruit of the Spirit!

"But the fruit of the Spirit is
love,
joy,
peace,
patience,
kindness,
goodness,
faithfulness,
gentleness,
self-control;
against such things there is no law."

Galatians 5:22-23

Love	Psalm 119:165
Joy	Ephesians 4:32
Peace	Philippians 4:5
Patience	Proverbs 25:28
Goodness	Proverbs 12:20
Kindness	Nahum 1:7
Faithfulness	1 John 4:12
Gentleness	Romans 8:25
Self-Control	Psalm 57:10

Let's take a closer look at this fruit!

LOVE

THE BIBLE HAS SO MANY SCRIPTURES ABOUT LOVE. FIND YOUR FAVORITE VERSE AND WRITE IT DOWN.

____

____

____

____

____

____

____

____

____

JOY

JOY

PEACE

PEACE

PATIENCE

WHAT DOES THE BIBLE HAVE TO SAY ABOUT PATIENCE?

KINDNESS

KINDNESS 

WHERE DO YOU FIND KINDNESS MENTIONED IN THE BIBLE?

GOODNESS

GOODNESS

FIND A SCRIPTURE ABOUT GOODNESS.

FAITHFULNESS

FAITHFULNESS

GOD HAS SO MUCH TO SAY ABOUT FAITHFULNESS IN HIS WORD!

GENTLENESS

GENTLENESS

Write out some of your favorite things you have read about gentleness in the Bible!

SELF-CONTROL

SELF-CONTROL

WHAT DOES THE BIBLE SAY ABOUT SELF-CONTROL?

Remember Paul? His name used to be Saul, and he was not a nice person at all. He was very mean to others. When he learned the truth about Jesus, he changed and became a nice person that was excited to tell everyone about Jesus! That is when he became known as Paul. He was full of joy, love, and kindness. He often had to be patient and also show self-control.

Paul experienced and was able to use the fruit of the Spirit for himself as he grew closer and closer to Jesus! You can read the amazing story of Paul in the book of Acts; chapter nine tells the story of how he came to know Jesus.

The Holy Spirit helped Paul use the fruit of the Spirit. The Holy Spirit will help you too! You will want to love others, show them kindness, and be joyful. You will be able to have peace no matter what your circumstances are. The Holy Spirit will also help you to be patient when waiting.

You can help other people grow fruit in their lives too! When you tell them about Jesus and they want to know Him and have Him in their life, they can grow the fruit of the Spirit just like you did. They will see the fruit in your life. They will see your love, joy, peace, patience, kindness, goodness, faithfulness, gentleness, and self-control.

SHARE THE FRUIT!

Not Just Any Old Fruit:
Picking the Fruit of the Spirit

Written and Illustrated By Emily Reagan
www.emilyreagan.com

Editor: Katherine Walton

ISBN: 979-8-9953244-0-9
Printed in the United States of America
©2026 By Emily Reagan

Joyful Press Publishing LLC
Spring Hill, Tennessee
www.joyfulpresspublishing.com